What is Happiness

and Where Can I get Some?

BONNIE MOEHLE

Edited By
Carly Goldberg

ISBN: 978-1-58776-902-3

Library of Congress catalog card number:

Manufactured in the United States of America

675 Dutchess Turnpike, Poughkeepsie, NY 12603
www.hudsonhousepub.com   (800) 724-1100

Dedication

For my Nanas Julia and Marcia who had long, full lives and passed away on the very same day.

For Julia
You were a shining example of unconditional love and acceptance. Your life was truly a demonstration of what it means to live from the inside out. You showed me that happiness does come from within. You inspired me.

For Marcia
Your honesty and sense of humor filled me with joy. Your never ending fountain of youth gave me inspiration. Your appreciation of the beautiful things that life has to offer opened me to the possibilities. You were a gift.

Acknowledgement

For Larry
Thank you for sharing your incredible talents.
I am so grateful.

Hap·pi·ness (noun)

A state of well-being and contentment

Table of Contents

Introduction

We are all One. We are One with Divine Intelligence and we are One with each other. We are all pieces of one Universal puzzle, every piece fluid and moving, each movement affecting all the other pieces of the puzzle. Every piece contains a different picture and yet one that fits perfectly with those around it. Each piece is a unique and individual expression of itself and yet an integral part of the whole. We are all Divine Intelligence expressing Self and having experiences through the vehicle of our humanness, through the use of the individual picture on a puzzle that would be incomplete without all of its pieces.

Being human is a gift. It gives us the opportunity to experience life – to taste a chocolate, to smell a rose, to hear a song or feel an emotion. This opportunity includes all aspects of life, not just those that feel good. We are here to have all of our experiences. Part of our journey is to stop judging those that feel uncomfortable. It is the judgment and the labeling of our experiences that causes our pain and prevents us from feeling our happiness.

Because most of us do not want to feel the uncomfortable experiences, we try to drive them away, to stuff them down or distract ourselves from them so that we don't have to deal with the pain. We hate the pain. But pain is here for us. It is like an alarm system alerting us to look inside of ourselves. We are here to embrace all of our emotions. And when we do, an angry moment becomes a bit of information – if we relax into the feeling instead of hating it. When we move into an uncomfortable feeling or a painful emotion instead of pushing it away, we experience the beautiful gift of being human.

We have forgotten who we are. We are whole and complete and we have everything we could possibly want or need within us. We have forgotten the Truth. Instead, we believe we are our thoughts. We have become completely identified with a role we play or a personality we have taken on. We are not our minds or our personalities; we are not our egos.

The ego is that part of us that uses thought to strengthen itself. The fearful ego believes it will die if it doesn't reinforce itself over and over again with negative thinking, so it cunningly convinces us to worry about the future, feel guilty about the past, and to blame others for the way we feel. The ego influences us to label our experiences as good or bad. However, there really is no good and bad. This is a perceived reality. Our ego is not who we really are. It is a perceived self, a facade we use to get what we think we need.

We are not our thoughts. When we see our thoughts for what they are – *just thoughts* – then we have peace. When we identify with the ego, we get so caught up in thought that our lives become unconscious. We become the thoughts. We have no awareness of how we're creating everything that we are experiencing and we continue on, day after day, feeling like a victim of our circumstance.

The only reason we don't experience who we truly are is this identification with thought that convinces us that we are less than perfect. Watch a small child who is not yet caught up in thought. There is no worry or fear or self-deprecation. There is only the joy of observing and experiencing life and the expression of self when a need arises. That is Awareness. That is who we are before thought, before identification with ego. That is happiness.

Prologue

☙ Where Does Happiness Come From?

We've all heard that happiness comes from within, but we don't quite know how to access it. So, we keep looking for it outside of ourselves in material possessions or validation from others. Sure, we get those temporary quick fixes, but not the everlasting happiness we are all yearning for.

What is the secret to happiness? When I first learned that it comes from within, I knew there was truth to that. I was excited about the concept, but that's all that it was – a concept. I had no idea how to apply it in any practical way. I thought if I could figure it out, I could help others. Then the answer came to me through awareness. As I continued to work on myself, my awareness

9

became very tuned in. I began to notice when I was happy and was able to observe the causes.

One day I was driving in my car feeling completely filled with joy. I asked myself, why am I feeling so happy? The first thing that came to me was this: I am pleased with myself. This is something that used to be difficult for me to say; there were times when it was hard for me to love myself. But after years of self awareness and growth, I've learned to love and fully accept myself regardless of what I am doing or accomplishing or what others are thinking of me. And I realized that self-love is one of the paths to happiness.

I then explored the question further. Why else am I happy? The second thing that came to my awareness is that I am constantly growing. I see every moment, even those that are difficult, as an opportunity for self improvement and spiritual growth. As a result, every situation is a valuable situation. And that makes me happy. I love my birthdays (and I'm over the half-century mark) because I know that each year is filled with opportunities to learn and grow, and that excites me. Did you know that the Chinese use the same word for crisis as they do for opportunity?

Upon further self exploration, I realized that I'm happy because I no longer hate "what is." Instead of wishing things were different, I embrace all of the moments in my life. When we no longer hate "what is" then even the uncomfortable times are simply an opportunity to have an experience. And we need all of our experiences. After all, how can we know joy if we don't know lack of joy? If we no longer hate the uncomfortable moments, then they are no longer difficult. They are simply experiences. We are here to have every experience, to live in the moment and be completely present to "what is." Life is about the journey, not the destination.

Finally, I realized that I am happy because I make time for gratitude every day, to look around

11

and say thank you for everything I have. I make it a practice to see through loving eyes. And I strive to love unconditionally without asking for anything in return. That brings me the greatest joy of all.

We have life backwards. We believe that if we accomplish a task or get what we want we will be happy. Sure, getting the things we want gives us temporary feelings of satisfaction, but they don't last. When we go inside ourselves to bring out our happiness, we find that we already have everything we've been searching for.

Part 1

Practicing Self-Love and Acceptance

It is impossible for us to be happy if we don't love and accept ourselves. Most of us have difficulty with self-love because we have very poor training. As a matter of fact, we have been conditioned *not* to love ourselves. Let's examine five of the reasons why we have such difficulty with self-love:

1. We have been taught that self-love is bad, that it makes us arrogant and conceited, that if we love ourselves we are no longer humble. But self love is not arrogant or conceited at all. Arrogance and conceit demand external validation. Self-love requires no external validation. Self-love is respectful to self *and* to others. It is non-judgmental. It takes nothing

15

personally and it sees others through the eyes of love and wisdom.

Note: humble does not mean that we should find fault with ourselves. It means that we surrender (let go of the illusion of control and allow life to flow).

2. We believe that self-love is conditional. We think we have to meet certain conditions in order to love ourselves. This starts when we are very young and we find ourselves being praised for some behaviors and punished for others. We develop this belief that love from others and self-love is dependent upon what we do. Then we only love ourselves when we get the good grade, are the cool kid in school, graduate with honors, make the sale, accomplish the task, etc. The problem with conditional self-love is that when we meet a condition, the feeling is only temporary, and then, within a very short period of time, there is another condition waiting for us to fulfill in order to feel self-love once again.

3. We have been taught that doing something well or being kind is expected, so we rarely focus on the kind and loving things we do innately. Instead we put our attention on the things that we do that we think are "bad." We beat ourselves up because we believe it will make us better. We focus on our perceived failures and our unmet expectations instead of loving ourselves for the beautiful things we do naturally *every* day.

4. We look for self-love outside of ourselves. We believe that the pat on the back from a boss, the compliments we get from a loved one, a raise in income, or a material possession will give us self-love and make us happy. We think that self-validation will come from what we have, what we do, and what others think of us. But it doesn't. Self-love is an inside job and all of those fore mentioned are external. They may feel good for a while, but they don't give us self-love. Self-love has to come from self.

17

5. Finally, we don't have self-love because we don't know the Truth of who we are. We believe we are separate from each other and separate from Divine Intelligence, and this belief in the separation creates the need to judge and compete and be better than. We see the world we live in as "us versus them." But we are not separate. We are connected to each other and to all of the knowledge of the Universe.

We think we are our egos and the ideas and beliefs that run around incessantly in our minds. We are completely mind-identified. But we are not our minds. The thoughts and beliefs we have were given to us by our predecessors and our past experiences. They are not who we are. We are whole and complete and have everything we could possibly want or need within us. We are love and acceptance, peace and abundance, joy and well-being. The reason we don't experience ourselves in this way is

because we think we are the experiences that
our thoughts create.

It's as if every day is a cloudy day. The sun is
always there, but it is masked by a cloud cover
of thought patterns and programs given to us by
others. Who we are is self-love and acceptance,
and that is always there. It is only thought that
prevents us from experiencing ourselves as
whole.

✑ Making a Commitment

So how do we move that cloud of thought out
of the way so that we can feel our wholeness and
love ourselves better? We first have to make a
commitment. Loving ourselves takes work at the
beginning, and even after it becomes more natural,
it is a life-long process. But self-love is worth it. It
brings peace and joy into our lives. When we lack
self-love, we are depriving ourselves of happiness

and creating the following types of conflict and pain for ourselves:

- The need to be right
- Taking the words and actions of others personally
- Blaming others for the way we feel
- Setting unhealthy boundaries
- Misperceiving the meaning of a comment as a criticism
- Becoming defensive
- The need for validation
- Making judgments of ourselves and others
- Beating ourselves up (second guessing ourselves)
- Feeling guilty
- Taking blame for the emotions of others
- Only liking people who agree with us

When we do the work and have healed our lack of self-love, these types of conflicts fade out of our lives. We see the world as a kinder, gentler place. People are no longer "out to get us," and we are much more trusting. We stop taking things personally, and we let go of the judgments of ourselves and others. We accept people and situations as they are, and we no longer get angry with ourselves for having an uncomfortable emotion. Life and relationships become more peaceful and joyful. Isn't that worth it?

Here's an example of the perceptions created by a lack of self-love. Two friends, Matt and Larry, were out walking. They both noticed a limousine parked in the driveway of a nearby house. Larry commented on how spoiled kids are today. They get to drive in limousines when he always had to walk. At that same moment, Matt had been thinking about how nice it was that somebody was going to have a romantic evening. Although they were looking at the same thing, they were seeing something completely different. Through Larry's eyes, the world they were walking in looked threatening and painful. To Matt, it was beautiful and loving.

Why the difference? Because of the filters

through which we see, filters that come from our past experiences. To those who see through the filters of judgment, those who find fault with themselves, the world is a harsh and unkind place. To those who love and fully accept themselves, the world is a beautiful place to live in.

What can we do then to heal that lack of self-love? Well, for starters, we have to align our thinking with who we are. Most people focus their thoughts about themselves on what they don't like or on what they believe they did wrong. Negative self-talk is aligned with a fearful ego, not with the Truth of who we are. What many of us are unaware of is that what we focus on and what we think about creates what we experience. This concept is true of everything. The experiences we have are the end result of what we spend most of our time thinking about.

It works like this: the subconscious mind is like a robot that *we* program. Whatever we tell it over and over again becomes an instruction. It takes the information we feed into it and spits it back out in the form of our perceptions, our behaviors, and then our outcomes. If we are in the habit of telling ourselves that we are not good enough, our subconscious mind will turn that into the perception that everybody is judging us. That perception will then become a behavior that turns people away. If we repeatedly think we'll never have enough money, the subconscious mind will give us perceptions of financial lack and the behaviors that prevent us from becoming prosperous. We won't even realize what we are doing. It is just a natural cause and effect. Beliefs create behaviors.

Many of my clients tell me that they never have enough time, so I ask them to do an experiment. I ask them to tell themselves that they have plenty of time and that everything gets done effortlessly – to think that way every day for three months. I tell them to do it diligently and to think it with feeling as if it were already true. After only weeks, they all come back to me with the same

23

results. They now have plenty of time and everything is getting done effortlessly. How is this possible? Beliefs create behaviors.

Our subconscious mind does its job and follows *our* instructions by influencing our behaviors to automatically follow our dominant thoughts. Our behaviors occur naturally as a consequence of what we are thinking. When we observe our thoughts, we can see a direct correlation between what we think and believe and the way we behave. Our experiences are the direct result of what we think.

We spend so much time in self-deprecating thinking and then wonder why we feel so unhappy. When we observe what we focus on when we think about ourselves, we find that we have a lot of negative self-talk. That self-talk creates an experience. When we spend most of our day thinking we're not good enough, someone can walk into a room and make a funny face and we interpret it as, "they think I'm not good enough."

Our beliefs create a perception that everyone is judging us. Are they? Or is it just a perception? We then react to the perception with defensiveness or aloofness. Then the people around us react back, strengthening the ego and the belief that we are not good enough. What we fail to see is that our belief created a perception which caused a reaction which created an outcome that confirmed the belief. Our perceptions and outcomes would be completely different if we focused more of our thoughts on loving and accepting ourselves. How can we possibly feel "good enough" when we are constantly putting ourselves down? A friend once told me that if he talked to his friends the way he talks to himself, he wouldn't have any friends.

We can change how we experience ourselves by changing what we think – by aligning our thoughts with the Truth of who we are which is whole and perfect. But we must stop beating ourselves up. It's simply a waste of time. It doesn't give us the result we think it will. It just holds us in the self-deprecating thought patterns that cause us to repeat the behaviors we are beating ourselves up over. What we focus on, we get more of. We beat ourselves up because we think it will make us better. That is an illusion. Beating ourselves up will not make us better. It will only make us beat ourselves up more.

✑ Aligning Ego with Truth

So, how do you align your ego with Truth? By changing the way you think, changing what you focus on. You can start by making a list. Write down five things you love about yourself.

For many people this is a difficult task. We are so conditioned to focus on what we don't love about ourselves that we have difficulty coming up with the things that we do love about ourselves.

Try some basics: I am kind, I am creative, I love to learn, I am honest with my friends, I love to laugh. See what you can come up with, but yes, make that list. Use it every day. Remind yourself of the items on the list as often as you can. Make it a discipline. Tell yourself while in the car, while in the shower. Think of it often. How can you experience self-love if you don't give love to yourself?

It's like building muscles. We know they're in there, but we can't see them until we pay attention to them and work on them on a regular basis. Our self-love is in there, but we have to pay attention to it and nurture it on a regular basis too. If we do, nobody else's judgment can hurt us, and life becomes so much more peaceful. Conflicts disappear. We feel happy.

Parents often ask me how they can help their children to be more confident. "Would it help if I tell them how wonderful they are every day?" Well, it helps, but nobody can give confidence to anybody else. We all have to get it from within. We would be much more effective in helping our children if every day we asked them what *they* love about themselves. We could help them to create a habit by making it a game; before they leave for school they tell us what they love about themselves. Then when the bully at school calls them a name, they aren't hurt, because they are so grounded in knowing who they are that the words of another mean nothing.

What else can we do to bring out our self-love, the true essence of who we are? We all have things that we innately do throughout the course of our day that are kind and loving. Stop taking those everyday moments for granted.

When you bring out someone else's laughter, love yourself for that. When you are nice to the person behind you in line at the grocery store, love yourself for that. When you are honest with a friend, love yourself for that. When you are a great listener, love yourself for that. Focus on the things that you already do every day and love them.

Remember, what we focus on is what we experience. Beliefs create behaviors. When we take the time to focus on what we love about ourselves during the course of our day, we feel happy.

Here's another tidbit that helps us bring out our self-love. Self-love naturally strengthens when we make it a practice to relinquish judgment, when we stop judging. It's an interesting phenomenon that when we love ourselves more, we become less judgmental, and when we judge less, we will love ourselves more.

So how do we let go of judgment in a world filled with judgment? Start by understanding that nothing anybody says or does is about you. The words and actions of others are about their fears, their needs, how they feel about themselves, and a collection of all of their experiences and the effects those experiences have had on them. If someone judges you, it's not about you; it's about their need to judge. We judge because it makes us feel better

29

about ourselves. If someone is angry at you, it's not about you; it's about the belief that anger will get you to change and will get them what they want. If someone acts loving toward you, that's not about you either. It's about the joy that they are getting from giving love.

Try turning the table so that you can really see the truth in this. Notice how nothing you do is about anybody else. Everything you do is to fill a need or to feel comfortable in a moment. Think about it.

Next, practice seeing through the eyes of love and wisdom. People behave the way they do because they are doing the best they can, with the tools they have so far, to feel comfortable in this crazy world. Take words like "lazy," "selfish," and "rude" out of your repertoire. Those are just words that humans created to use for manipulating others in order to get what they want. When you see through the eyes of love and wisdom, you see the underlying causes of someone's behavior rather than labels and judgments.

How does relinquishing judgment bring out self-love? Here's a story to demonstrate. When my daughter was younger, I took her to the hair salon. When we walked into the salon, the energy was very negative and the girls working there were all acting quite nasty. I could see that the gal who was scheduled to cut my daughter's hair was the instigator of this situation. My daughter was pulling on my shirt and asking to leave. "Mom, please don't let that nasty woman cut my hair. She'll mess it up." In that moment, it would have been so easy for me to make a judgment and walk out of the salon. But instead, I chose to see through the eyes of love and wisdom.

The next thing I knew, I was asking the hair professional, "Are you okay?" She took in a very deep breath, let it out slowly and said, "Thank you so much for asking. I have a bad back, my insurance doesn't cover the cost of the surgery I

31

need, and as a single mom I can't afford to pay for it myself." She went on to explain that the only work she felt qualified to do hurt her back and made it worse. This morning she had awakened in terrible pain and was very frightened. Now, everyone in the salon was being so mean to her too. (Of course, they were making her actions about them and reacting, and that's why they seemed mean).

I looked at her kindly and told her that I was so sorry for what she was going through. At that moment, she melted. She gave my daughter a free deep conditioning and was very nice to be around. In addition, the energy of the entire salon shifted.

As I said, it would have been so easy to have made a judgment and stormed out of the salon. Instead, I chose to relinquish judgment and to love and serve. Not only did relinquishing judgment help everyone in the salon transform, but I transformed too. I felt wonderful about myself. I loved myself. And I felt happy.

As we practice self-love, we begin to take better care of ourselves. We find the time to eat right and exercise and care for our bodies. We do the things we love to do without feeling guilty about it. We play and become more creative and feel unafraid to act on our desires and inspirations. We take time for a quiet moment or stop to take in the world around us. We laugh more and even act silly. We become more childlike and less cynical. We naturally and easily balance our lives better. We feel more capable and confident. And we have the energy and the motivation to serve others without feeling obligated or resentful. What could be better than that?

Seeing Every Situation as an Opportunity

Everything is exactly as it is supposed to be. When we trust in this, life flows and we see every moment as an opportunity to have an experience, and every experience as an opportunity to expand or to let go. We're lucky too. We have an internal guidance system that lets us know when to let go.

However, we also have an ego. The ego is that part of us that makes the interpretations which determine whether an experience is pleasant or unpleasant. Unfortunately, for almost all of us, the ego has been trained to be fearful and it uses negative thought to strengthen itself. It is very afraid of change, so it will do its best to keep us repeating our painful patterns. If we engage in anxious or self-deprecating thinking, the ego will do everything in its power to hold us there by convincing us that we will get something out of it. The ego always has to be right. It believes that if we release old patterns, it will die. That is why we have such a hard time letting go of the way we think, even when our thoughts cause us pain. But the ego doesn't die, it transforms.

To transform the ego we have to listen to the internal guidance system from within our bodies. It is the voice inside of us that lets us know when we are identifying with or strengthening our ego. I call this voice the Internal Teacher. The Internal Teacher communicates to us through the feelings in our body. When we are strengthening our egos by identifying with fearful thinking, the Internal Teacher gives us pain, or an uncomfortable feeling inside. This feeling is an alarm system alerting us to thoughts that are aligned with our ego rather than with the Truth of who we are.

How can you use your alarm system? When you catch yourself worrying about the future, notice how your body feels. More than likely, it feels tense or anxious. That feeling is the alarm going off, a message from the Internal Teacher. The message is something like this, "Hey, Internal Teacher here. I'm giving you this uncomfortable feeling to get your attention. I want to let you know that the thought you're identifying with, the one about the future, the one you just made up and are completely caught up in, well, you might want to consider letting it go. Why? It's strengthening your fearful ego and taking away your energy and clarity. And it's not aligned with who you are." The uncomfortable feeling you have when you are worrying about the future is simply a message. It is there to help you.

When you are finding fault with yourself, you may notice that your body feels tired and run-down. There's that Internal Teacher again, giving you a message. "Hey, Internal Teacher here, giving you some discomfort to remind you that the thought you're identifying with is not aligned with the Truth of who you are."

Life wants us to be happy. That is why it gave us an Internal Teacher. Listen to it. It takes some practice and a great degree of self-awareness. As a matter of fact, I used to believe that when I had an uncomfortable feeling in my body that it was a confirmation that my thoughts were true. But I had it backwards. Every time we feel emotional discomfort in our bodies, our Internal Teacher is guiding us back to happiness by alerting us to the thoughts that take it away from us.

What is the opportunity that the Internal Teacher is pointing us to? I hear this question asked often. "If the pain from the Internal Teacher is a message, then what is the message?"

The message is this: Look at yourself and observe the thinking patterns and programs that are taking away your peace and happiness, the programs that cause you to react to life the way you do.

Where do these thought patterns and programs come from? Our past experiences, the people and situations we grew up with, our teachers and environments, and the behaviors that were modeled to us. And why do we hold onto them even though they take away our peace and bring us pain? Because we believe that if we behave the way we do, we will get what we want.

✑ Understanding the Causes

There are five underlying causes for our behaviors and reactions and they trigger our Internal Teacher so that we can observe and then heal them. Understanding and identifying them creates an opportunity to grow spiritually. When we take that opportunity and run with it, we feel joy, even in the midst of a challenging emotion.

41

Let's take a look at the **Five Underlying Causes for Pain**:

1. We have pain because **we believe we're not good enough**. The belief that we're not good enough creates so many conflicts and misperceptions. As I mentioned earlier, when we believe we are not good enough, we take things personally, set unhealthy boundaries, find fault with ourselves, have the need for outside validation, etc…

   The next time you take something personally, take notice of how your body feels. Of course it is going to feel uncomfortable. That's your Internal Teacher talking to you. What's it telling you? That your thoughts and reactions are not Truth and that if you want to stop reacting to others in ways that cause you pain, then you'll have to start loving yourself. By the way, nobody causes your pain. It is the reaction you have to them that causes your pain, and the underlying belief that you're not good enough that causes your reaction.

2. We also have pain because **we have attachments** or expectations we are unable to let go of. What's an attachment? We all have visions in our minds of how the people and situations in our lives should look. When things don't happen the way we want them to, we get stressed. It seems as though the stress we feel is caused by the people in our lives not meeting our expectations, or by situations not working out the way we want them to.

This is not true. The pain we feel is the Internal Teacher pointing out an inability to accept things as they are. If our computer stops working in the middle of a project, it is not the computer causing our pain. It is the non-acceptance of "what is" and the fear that things won't get done that cause the pain. If a husband calls his wife a half an hour later than he said he would and she feels angry, he did not cause

43

her anger. It is the attachment she had to how he should behave, or the fact that she took it personally, that caused her anger. Besides, that anger is just a reaction. We use anger to try to manipulate others to make them stop their behavior so that we won't have to take responsibility for our reaction to it.

So often we think that our pain is caused by someone else's behavior and if they would just change then we wouldn't feel the pain. We even try to control them or name-call to get rid of the pain; but we can't change "what is" and we can't ask an oak tree to be a pine tree. Our pain is not caused by someone else's behavior. It is caused by an attachment we have to how they behave and an inability to let go of that attachment. They are just being exactly who they are. It is only our need for them to be the way we want them to be that causes the pain.

We try to control situations so that we don't have to deal with letting go if things don't work out according to planned. We schedule every moment and predetermine every step hoping that the outcome will be exactly as we had anticipated. This creates stress because we try so hard to make things look the way we think they should look, and when they don't, there is disappointment and upset. When we let go of our attachments, everything flows perfectly and there is no longer a need to control. Instead, there is an excitement about the possibilities to come and an enjoyment and appreciation of the moment we're in.

The Internal Teacher is always there to tell us when we are holding onto an attachment. The next time you are feeling emotional discomfort, ask yourself if you are resisting "what is." Do you want to change or control something that you can't?

The Internal Teacher wants to help us let go of all of our attachments. Attachments will always set us up for the possibility of pain.

They will also limit us. When we are attached to how someone or something is, it's like having blinders on. We become so focused on how we think things have to be that we become incapable of seeing that there are other possibilities. We miss opportunities to try something new because our need for certainty and control make it impossible to see what else is right in front of us, something that may be even better.

What are our choices when things aren't going the way we want them to? We can accept and allow "what is" to be "what is" and be at peace within ourselves. We can hate "what is" and constantly fight the people and situations in our lives. Or we can leave those people or situations. The only problem with leaving is if we haven't accepted first, we will surely experience the same problems again somewhere else. If we fully accept, and let go of our attachments, we may no longer wish to leave. When we let go of our attachments, we no longer have resistance to what happens in our lives. Without resistance, we have happiness.

Let's say we go to the grocery store and we really want a specific brand of pickles, but they are out of our pickles. The pain we feel is not because the store manager didn't do his job and order pickles. The pain we feel comes from our inability to let go of our attachment to the pickles. We now have choices: 1) we can accept that they are out of pickles, which will open us up to trying something new (perhaps coleslaw?), 2) we can continue to hate "what is" and yell at the store manager, which will not get us our pickles and will take away our peace, 3) we can leave the store angry, or 4) we can kindly tell the store manager that they are out of pickles and leave peacefully knowing we have accepted "what is." In letting go of an attachment, we make the choices that are accepting and peaceful rather than those that rob us of our happiness.

Keep in mind that acceptance is not defeat. We always have choices. Acceptance is a way to bring peace into the moment. Once we have accepted, we can make much clearer choices because they come from a space of clarity rather than a space of anger and judgment.

3. The third reason we have pain is because **we regret the past**. We feel guilty, we beat ourselves up, we "would have, should have, could have," and we rehash the past.

Remember the last time you were beating yourself up about something you did earlier that day? How was your body feeling? Pretty low energy would be my guess.

That uncomfortable feeling we get when we beat ourselves up is the Internal Teacher alerting us to remind ourselves that our self-talk is aligned with our ego rather than our Truth. It is guiding us away from the thoughts we are having. Besides, the belief that beating ourselves up will make us better is a big lie. Remember, beliefs create behaviors, and if we believe that we are no good then we will create more of the same behaviors as the ones that we are beating ourselves up over.

So <u>CUT IT OUT</u>!

Guilt feels painful. That's because guilt will not make us better people and will not change what already happened. The Internal Teacher will guide us away from guilt. The Internal Teacher knows that happiness and peace cannot exist in regret of the past, so it will give us pain to point us away from the past. What I have discovered, is that rehashing the past is not necessary – ever! There are only two reasons that serve us to go into the past. One is to learn about our own thoughts and reactions and the feelings that they've created so that we can shift them if they caused us pain. The other reason to go into the past is to use a memory to experience a feeling. If we remember a joyful time from our past, we can re-experience the feeling it brought us. Other than those two reasons, the past is unnecessary. The only place for peace is in the Present moment. That is where we need to be.

4. The fourth reason we feel pain is because **we fear the future**. We "what if" about everything and become stressed out and worried about things that don't even exist. In any situation there are infinite possibilities as to the future outcome, and yet we find one to glom onto based on our past and we obsess over it, creating a great level of anxiety inside of ourselves. This feeling of anxiety or stress is the Internal Teacher reminding us that our thoughts of "what if" are not aligned with truth but are instead strengthening our egos. If we want to feel peace, the only answer is to be aware or our own thought processes and to talk ourselves out of them. What I always do whenever my Internal Teacher is pointing out my "what iffing" is I remind myself that the thoughts that are creating my pain are just made

up; they don't even exist. Then I laugh at my own ego and pull myself into the moment by using my senses to listen or to feel. Presence comes from fully experiencing every smell, every taste, every touch, every sound, right now. This always takes me out of the pain and stress of worrying about the future, the pain that I just created with *my* mind.

Something as common as feeling overwhelmed is a fear of the future too. The reason we feel overwhelmed is because the moment we get a large list of things to do, the mind immediately starts to focus on fear. "What if I don't get this all done," "What if I forget something," "What if there isn't enough time?" And so on. But it is not the list that is causing the stressful feeling. It is the Internal Teacher alerting us to our fearful thinking that causes the feeling. It is how we are reacting to and thinking about the list that is causing the feeling.

51

There are people who have similar lists and challenges in life but never feel overwhelmed because they don't "what if" about their lists. Instead, they turn their thoughts to, "I know this will all get done in perfect time," and they go about life, allowing things to flow naturally (as they do when we let go of the fear of the future).

5. The fifth reason we have pain is that **we are not in integrity with ourselves**. We say yes when we'd really rather say no, and we tell lies with the intention of sparing someone's feelings. Then we wonder why we never have authentic, honest relationships. But let's understand why we do this. We are not in integrity with ourselves because we are afraid. We're afraid that others won't love us, and we need others to love us because we don't love ourselves enough. We say that we lie to avoid conflict, but in reality, we are just afraid that the people in our lives will be angry and then they won't

love us, and again, we need to be loved by others because we don't love ourselves enough.

When we say yes when we'd really rather say no, we do it because we want to feel like a good person or we want to avoid hurting someone. The difficulty is that we end up resenting the people we are trying to please and eventually pushing them away. It feels as though the pain we feel when we are resentful was caused by the person who asked for the favor. "If that jerk didn't ask me to do that chore for him then I wouldn't feel this way." But the pain is really just the Internal Teacher, once again, pointing out that we are aligned with our egos rather than the Truth of who we are.

Many of us are unaware that true honesty never hurts anyone. Sure, others may react to our honesty with hurt, but we did not cause their hurt. They have Five Underlying Causes for their pain too. When they are hurt, it is only because one or more of their five is coming up to be looked at. When we see through the eyes of love and wisdom, we recognize this. The people in our lives may not know or be aware of this information, but if we spend our lives protecting everyone we know from their pain (so that they will love us) we'll be walking on eggshells. What a horrible feeling. And, by protecting others, we prevent *them* from opportunities for self-improvement and spiritual growth.

Note: honesty is not an excuse to be unkind. True honesty has no agenda.

✑ Turning Pain into Opportunity

So, how do we turn these five reasons for pain into opportunities? Here's an exercise that will help you make use of them:

In order to do this exercise, you must **stop blaming** others for how you feel. Blame comes from a lack of understanding of the true source of emotional pain. Blame is the belief that someone or some situation caused the pain. Now that you know that the causes of your pain are within you, make a decision from this day forward to no longer blame anyone else for how you feel. Nobody else caused your pain. It is your Five Underlying Causes that triggered the pain. If you go on blaming others, you remain a powerless victim and the people and situations in your life have the power to determine how you feel.

When you stop blaming, you become empowered. You also must stop blaming yourself. Blaming yourself will not make you better; it will only recreate more of the same behaviors. So no blaming yourself either! Instead, look to your Five Underlying Causes as the reasons for your suffering. By looking at those five causes, you can identify the message your pain is giving you and use the pain instead as an opportunity to affect change. When the pain comes up, identify which of your Five Underlying Causes is showing itself to you, and recognize, "Oh, there's number two again. I have an attachment I'm not letting go of. No wonder I'm in pain." Once you recognize where the pain is coming from, you are beginning the process of healing.

Now that you have made a commitment to stop blaming, the next step in the exercise is to **listen to your Internal Teacher**. Every time your body feels uncomfortable, acknowledge that you are getting a message from your Internal Teacher. I even talk to myself. "I'm feeling emotional discomfort in my body. Ok, Internal Teacher, I understand that you are trying to tell me something. You are reminding me that my thinking is not aligned with who I Am. I hear you. I'll take a look at my thoughts. Thank you for the message." Sounds silly, I know. But we talk to ourselves all of the time about very self-destructive things. Why not talk to yourself this way instead? It is a great way to begin the process of releasing painful patterns.

Listening to and acknowledging the Internal Teacher is an important step. It creates an internal shift by minimizing the energy of the ego. I can explain it like this: when my children were small, we would spend time at the park with other moms and their kids. The moms would sit and chat while the kids would play. When the kids wanted our attention they would holler out, "mom look at me, look at me, look at me!" Once they felt acknowledged and attended to, they would go back to their play, leaving us to continue talking.

Just like the children, the Internal Teacher needs to be acknowledged and attended to. If we ignore the Internal Teacher, it will continue to bring us pain just as a child would continue to shout "look at me!" This is why we have repeating painful patterns, because we don't listen to our Internal Teacher. By acknowledging that it is there to give us information, we let it know we hear it. Once it knows it has been heard, it begins to let us go, and the energy of the pain lessens.

Once you've acknowledged your Internal Teacher, see if you can **identify the thoughts** that created the pain. The moment we identify the thoughts that are causing our pain, we disconnect from the control of the ego and become the observer of the ego instead. As the observer, we begin to see how the ego operates to strengthen itself, and the magnitude of the pain again lessens.

Then **identify which of the Five Underlying Causes are showing themselves to you**. There may be more than one. Here's an example: I was working with a gal, let's call her Jan, who always felt tension whenever she was around her sister. Jan had always believed that the source of the tension was her sister Gail's criticisms, judgments and anger. Jan had been seeing herself as a victim. Once she let go of blame and began this exercise, Jan became aware that it was her belief that she was not good enough (underlying cause #1) and her unwillingness to let go of an attachment (underlying cause #2) that were the real causes for her pain – not Gail.

By recognizing this, Jan could now change her reactions toward her sister. She was now aware that it was her lack of self-love that created some of the hurt, so she began to work on self-love and acceptance. She was also able to see that her desire for her sister to be different was triggering a message. Jan had an attachment to how her sister behaved; she wanted the oak tree to be a pine tree. She wanted her sister to be less judgmental and angry. But that's how Gail was, and she wasn't going to change.

So Jan learned to love unconditionally and allow her sister to be exactly who she was. After that, Jan's relationship with Gail became joyful. Jan no longer took the words of her sister personally, and she no longer needed her sister to be different. Jan now feels wonderful about herself, and that brings out her happiness. In addition, Gail has changed too. Nobody keeps up a behavior unless they're getting something out of it. When Jan's reactions toward Gail changed, Gail began to communicate to Jan differently. It was a win-win for both of them.

When we identify one or more of our Five Underlying Causes showing themselves to us, we can take responsibility for our own reactions and change our life's experiences. Often times we will have more than one come up in any given painful moment. Stress may be caused by a fear of the future, but also by the belief that we're not good enough to handle things. Anger may be caused by an inability to let go of an attachment, but also by not being in integrity with ourselves. Feeling hurt by another may be the result of our "I'm not good enough stuff," but it may also be an inability to let go of an attachment. The healing process begins when we observe ourselves when we're in pain and then identify the underlying causes.

The next part of the exercise is to **feel the feelings** that the underlying causes leave in your body. Yes, feel them. Put all of your attention on the way you feel. If your heart is racing then feel it race. If your body is tense then feel the tension. If your stomach is knotted then feel the knots.

The reason we have so much repeated pain, the reason we have addictions and seek out external gratification, is because we never deal with our feelings in a healthy way. We label them as bad, then just bury them or distract ourselves from them.

Don't hate your discomfort. It is a message. Stop judging it or trying to push it away. Rather than seeing your feelings as good or bad, just see them as a lump in the throat or a tightness in the chest. Sit with the feelings. Embrace them as a message or an experience. Acknowledge the Internal Teacher. Then identify the underlying causes for the feelings and feel them. Refrain from revisiting the story that caused the feelings. Just Move right into them. FEEL them. When you put your attention on an uncomfortable feeling, it moves away. It may sound scary or even counter intuitive, but try it. By putting all of your attention on the feelings, you are no longer entertaining the thoughts that created them, and the feelings lift.

This works very well with anxiety. The next time you feel anxiety, acknowledge the Internal Teacher, identify the thoughts and underlying causes of the emotion, and then feel the anxiety. You can do it by first describing the feeling: "it feels like my heart is racing, my shoulder muscles are tight, and my hands are clenched and clammy." Then move into the feeling. Feel your heart racing. Feel the tightness in your shoulders. Put all of your attention on your clenched and clammy hands. Don't be frightened of it. Don't think about it, just fully experience it.

Most of us do not put our full attention on the feeling. We continue to energize the anxiety by putting our attention on the fearful thoughts that intensify the feeling. You must focus <u>FULLY</u> on the feeling. Continue to describe the feeling, and then move into it. You will notice that each time you describe and then feel the feeling, it will lessen until it either goes away or significantly lightens up – and it will. Try it. Most people don't want to do this. It's frightening to feel your feelings. But once you've tried it a few times, you will find that it is a very effective way to release your emotions. It will even work if you can't identify the thoughts creating the feeling.

◈ Changing Your Thoughts

The final step in the exercise is to **change your thoughts and perceptions**. This can be very difficult. We have a hard time changing the way we think and react because we don't want to let go of the payoff we get. In addition, the ego is always striving to prove itself right so it will justify everything we think. For example, we justify stress by convincing ourselves it will motivate us. Worry makes us more caring, and finding fault with ourselves makes us better.

The truth is, stress is an energy and clarity zapper, worry sends a message to the person we are worrying about that they need to be worried about and dis-empowers them, and finding fault with ourselves lowers our energy, making it impossible for us to move forward. The payoff we think we get from holding onto a thought or belief is simply a justification from the ego that holds us in the same patterns.

I was working with a woman who had fibromyalgia. I asked her what her payoff was from holding onto the fibromyalgia. After a long silence, she told me that the fibromyalgia brought her sympathy. Her husband was willing to help her more if she was in pain. In addition, the fibromyalgia gave her a sense of relief. If she didn't get things done, she could blame the fibromyalgia and that way she wouldn't have to beat herself up.

I asked her to evaluate the payoff. Would it be better to get sympathy and relief from her illness, or would it be better for her to love herself so that she could ask for help when she needed it and praise herself for taking a needed day off. In addition, self-love would give her the energy to get more done. Guess which payoff she picked?

Evaluate your payoffs and decide if they are really worth it. Then change your thoughts. Think about what you want rather than what you don't want. Change your self-talk and be self-loving rather than critical. Focus on what you have rather than what you don't have. Be in gratitude. See through the eyes of love and wisdom. See the perfection in those around you, and love them unconditionally. Use an affirmation, an "I Am" statement. "I Am" is a very powerful creation statement. Change your thoughts to align them with the Truth of who you are – whole, loving, peaceful, accepting and creative. When your thoughts are aligned with Truth, your body feels peaceful or energized.

As a single mother, I used to worry constantly about money. One day my daughter came home to announce that her glasses had broken, and she needed new contacts. At that very moment, I was opening the mail to find my biggest bills of the month. I started to feel very anxious and fearful, but I chose to use the moment as an opportunity. First I acknowledged that the uncomfortable feeling I was having was a message from my Internal Teacher letting me know that my reaction was not aligned with Truth. Second, I identified what I was thinking and realized that my fears of the future were coming to the surface to be looked at.

At this point I was beginning to feel relief from the fear, but I was still holding it in my body. So, I felt the feeling. I described it like little men trying to punch their way out from the inside. Then I put all of my attention on the feeling. I described the feeling again, only this time the little men were not punching as hard. I put all my attention on the feeling once more. I continued to repeat this procedure until the feeling disappeared. Then I changed my thoughts. It was easy to do because I had released the fearful emotions. My new thoughts were something like this: "The Universe always provides. I always have more than enough. I am so grateful for the money that I have to pay these bills. And I am abundant!"

Fear around money had been a deep seated issue for me. As a matter of fact, I used to dread going to the mailbox for fear that there might be a big bill waiting there. Over the years, I continued to use the steps described, peeling away the layers of old programming, until one day I went to the mailbox and my reaction was, "Oh, a bill? No problem. I always have enough." The pain that came from worrying about my bills had given me the opportunity to transform my fear into a new realization of abundance.

Use every situation as an opportunity. If you stop blaming people and situations for how you feel, and listen to your Internal Teacher, you will recognize the underlying causes for your pain. You will see the thoughts and programs that strengthen your ego and prevent your joy, and you will be able to release them and reprogram them. Each time you do, you will feel a sense of accomplishment, for you will have peeled away at the thinking that has prevented you from experiencing your joy.

One final note: If you use the exercise and you continue to have discomfort in your body, painful emotions that you are unable to release and thoughts that you cannot change, then just observe them – watch them. Sometimes it feels like our emotions are stuck inside, and they won't move away. That's okay. Eventually they will. So, don't hate your emotions, don't judge them, and don't wish they weren't there. Just let them be there. If you hate them, it will only serve to magnify the pain.

Instead, experience the thoughts and emotions. Watch them like you are watching a movie.

Embrace them. Embrace every feeling, every thought, every moment. We are here to experience life – *all* of it. You can't know light if you don't understand lack of light, and you can't know peace if you don't understand lack of peace. Everybody gets stuck in a "funk" sometimes. If you have a tough day, or even a tough week, that's okay. Find the joy even in the pain. Pain is a gift that points us back to who we truly are by showing us what we are not.

Part 3

℘ *Saying Yes to What Is*

We have so much resistance to the situations in our lives, and then we wonder why we're not happy. What is resistance? It is a non acceptance of "what is." When we hate "what is" we have pain. Resistance is the ego at work. The true Self is acceptance. The true Self allows life to flow and doesn't need to have it any different than it is. The ego always thinks that wherever we are or whatever is happening right now is not acceptable. It believes that we "should" be somewhere else or that some other time out in the future will be better than *now*.

To experience happiness, we have to let go of the need to control, let go of the need for certainty and "just say yes" to what is. Right after the 9/11 attack on the Twin Towers occurred, I heard Tony

Robbins in an interview say, "The quality of life is directly proportional to the amount of uncertainty that you can live with." And he was right. When we can trust that everything is exactly as it's supposed to be and just flow with what life brings us, we have peace and joy. The more we resist the flow of life and need it to be different than it is, the more pain we experience.

I once heard a story (I believe it came from the Taoist tradition) about a monk who would jump into the bottom of a raging waterfall every morning. The local villagers would watch him, questioning why he would torture himself in this way. Finally, one of the villagers asked the monk what he was doing and what would motivate him to jump into the treacherous water day after day. The monk went on to explain that the first few times he had tried it he fought the mighty water, coughing and choking and nearly drowning. But when he let go and just flowed with the water, his experience of the waterfall became one of joy and wonderment. That is why he now jumps in

74

everyday. Life is a journey, not a destination. When we let go of resistance and experience every moment, even the painful ones, then the journey is filled with adventure and opportunity.

✍ Practicing Presence

How do we let go of control and resistance so that we can experience the joy and wonderment of life? – By experiencing the present moment. **In the present moment there are no problems** or issues. There is just "what is." "What is" only becomes a problem when we start to think about it or judge it. We attach thoughts of the past or the future to our present moment and then we end up in regret or fear, and this creates pain.

When you feel that pain, recognize that it is the resistance to *now* that is causing it. Regretting the past or feeling guilty pulls you out of the present moment and will only cause you to repeat the past.

75

Here's a story about a man who repeated an unpleasant situation over and over again simply because he kept going back into his past. When he was a boy, his mother sent him to the department store to return an item. The woman at the return counter was very unkind to him and so he got this idea that being unkind was a prerequisite for the job. From that time on, he consistently had an unpleasant experience returning things. The people at the return counters were always unkind.

Once he learned to look at himself as the possible cause, he came to realize that he kept recreating that experience. His beliefs were affecting his behaviors. Because he expected the people at the return counters to be mean, he behaved in a very defensive way. They reacted to his defensiveness, and sure enough, they were mean. When he released the past and approached every new return as if he had never experienced it before, he found that his experience was completely different.

Worrying about the future also causes problems. When we worry about the future we are making things up in our minds that don't even exist. These worries create a perception of difficulty that isn't even there. This perception causes stress and takes away our joy. When we stay in the present moment, there are no problems. Sure, there may be uncomfortable moments, but they only become problems when we attach the past or the future to them.

Let's say you're sick. Being sick is not a problem. It just is "what is." It only becomes a problem when you think about how the last time you were sick it lasted for five days and your boss got angry with you and *what if* this time you're sick for five days and you get fired and become homeless and die!?

We think thoughts of the past and future and suddenly something that is a human experience becomes a major dilemma. But the mind created this dilemma. In the present moment there is never a problem; there is only "what is."

In the present moment life is filled with miracles. We feel every touch, taste every taste and hear every sound. We experience life the way we were meant to experience it, through the eyes of a very young child.

Have you ever observed toddlers? They coo and giggle, and when they fall down, they let out a loud cry that only lasts a few seconds. Then they are right back to cooing and giggling. This is presence. They are experiencing everything they see and hear, and it is all a miracle. Then when they fall down and feel pain they are present to that too. They don't hate or judge the pain. They don't try to push it away or deny its existence. They don't even think about it. They feel it fully, and in a short time it's gone. Then they go right back to experiencing the miracles around them. Imagine the joy you would feel if you fully experienced every moment, even the pain, without thought or judgment.

Because we are always in the past or in the future, we are living life in a constant illusion. In other words, most of us spend most of our time in the past (which no longer exists) or in the future (which doesn't yet exist). We're missing life. We're never experiencing what is happening right *now* because we are so caught up in the past and future thoughts that are running through the mind. We don't realize that the only thing that is real is what we are feeling, seeing, touching, right *now*. All of the rest doesn't exist. It's just a thought.

So walk across the room and feel the carpeting beneath your feet. Stand out in the sun and feel the warmth on your shoulders. Listen to the sounds outside your window. Those are the miracles. And every moment of your life can be filled with them if you are present.

In the present moment we get everything we need in the moment we need it. Life becomes effortless, everything just flows. Sure we live in a linear society, so we do have to schedule a meeting and book a flight, but the rest of the time, live in the present. When we do, we find that we get incredible moments of inspiration; we know things we didn't even know we knew and our creativity flows like never before. Being present is like being "in the zone" for an athlete. When an athlete gets the mind out of the way and stops thinking about the past or the future, that athlete plays at the top of his/her game. But as soon as that same athlete starts thinking about the last mistake or the next move, the momentum is lost.

We believe that we need to figure everything out with our minds. We try to control outcomes and the steps leading us there. What we don't realize is that if we just let go through presence, we will get all of the answers we need when we need them. The problem is that we don't trust, so we worry and regret and attempt to control,

80

thinking that if we don't our lives will fall apart. By living in the present moment, we no longer have to worry and control. We get everything we need when we need it. This is **surrender**. Surrender means getting out of our heads through presence so that if an answer is necessary we can hear it. Sometimes we hear nothing because presence is the answer. There are no problems in presence.

In the past, when you were overwhelmed with worry, has anybody ever suggested that you give it to God, or that you let go and let God? What does this mean? It means that you surrender through presence. It means that you move into the moment and let go of your worry-filled thoughts by practicing presence. When you do this, the answers come to you and they are better than any answers your limited mind could have manufactured.

Make presence a practice. As you go through your day, use all of your senses. Feel the steering wheel of the car in your hands as you drive. See the street out in front of you and listen to the lyrics of the song on the radio. When you lie in bed at night, feel the mattress beneath your body and the sheet above. Listen to the sounds in the room. Be fully present. You will know when you are fully present because there will be no thought or judgment. You will not be evaluating the situation. You will simply be experiencing it. Some people tell me that practicing presence is boring. But if you are fully present you can't possibly be bored. You are experiencing everything around you, and that is miraculous!

Presence may only last for a few seconds because the mind hates presence. It cannot operate in presence. In presence there is no thought. So the mind will do everything it can to convince us to think and to pull us out of the moment. As soon as you notice that you are thinking again, just pull yourself back into presence. It gets easier with practice.

Because the mind hates presence it will convince

us that presence is non-productive, a waste of time. It has us believing that we better think or our life will turn to chaos. If we practice presence, what we find is that it brings peace, and life does not fall apart. In fact, we get better answers through presence. Why? When we use the mind to figure everything out we are limiting ourselves.

The mind is fearful and only knows what it has seen or heard or read in our lifetime. Therefore, the answers it will come up with are fear based and limited. When we surrender through presence, the mind is no longer giving us the answers. They are coming from our connection with All That Is. Those answers will sometimes amaze us or be beyond our wildest dreams. But we can't possibly hear them if we are constantly thinking. They can only come through the silence and surrender of presence.

I have had many moments when I'm working with clients where I am asked a question that my ego does not know the answer to. When I stop trying to figure it out, when I stay quiet and just wait, the answer comes and it is always much better than any answer my mind could have come up with. It is always the perfect answer for the client. I discover that I know things I didn't even know I knew. Presence allows Right answers to come through. I love when that happens.

So stop hating what is. Just say yes. Instead of resisting, be present and fully experience the moment. Embrace the joyful times and the painful ones too. Then life becomes a journey filled with miracles and inspiration, and every moment is an opportunity.

Part 4

⚓ Living with Gratitude

Look around. Life has so much beauty and we are a part of it. We get so caught up in our heads thinking about yesterday and tomorrow that we miss the chance to revel in today. There is so much to be grateful for, even when life is difficult. We always have ourselves and our abilities regardless of what is happening around us. Be grateful for that. The rest is icing. So often we spend our time focusing on what is wrong or on what we don't have. We've been trained to do that. Our popular culture and the way we speak promotes that. We believe that by putting our attention on the things we don't have, somehow we will get them. "I'll never have that vacation" is not going to get us a vacation.

We have free will, the ability to think whatever

we want. But know that all thought creates perceptions, behaviors and outcomes. We reap what we sow The Universe cooperates with us. If we constantly think "I don't have" then the Universe will give us more "don't have." If we are living in gratitude, not only do we feel wonderful because we are always appreciating what is in front of us, but we also create more of it. When we repeatedly think "I have" then the Universe brings us more "have." Sometimes it comes in the form of an inspiration, a creative idea, a connection with the right person, good luck, or a knock on the door (to name a few). We are creators, and what we focus on, we get more of. So be grateful!

Now, bear in mind that we cannot control the thoughts that pop into our heads. Thoughts are energy and they just pop in. Have you ever noticed a thought and wondered where it came from? It felt as though it wasn't even your thought? We pick up on other people's thoughts. The thoughts that come in will come in. The questions is, are we identifying with those thoughts and getting emotionally tied to them, or are we recognizing them and seeing them for what they are – thoughts.

As our awareness heightens, we catch our thoughts earlier and earlier. We notice the feelings they create in the body, and that alerts us to the thoughts that are not aligned with the Truth of who we are. It is through this observation and awareness that change happens.

Don't hate your thoughts and don't judge them. If you do, they will repeat. Just embrace the thoughts and the feelings that accompany them. Observe them. And be grateful for the awareness. As you observe and embrace the painful thoughts and feelings, you will naturally release them. Then you can change what you are thinking and create what you want. You have the ability to manifest. We manifest what we put our attention on. What are you putting your attention on?

If your attention is on gratitude, you will continue to experience more of what you are grateful for, and you will feel happy. Every morning before you get out of bed, be grateful. Think about what you have. Appreciate nature. Take in every sight and sound. Feel every touch. Gratitude leads to joy, and the energy of joy puts us in the effortless flow rather than the path of resistance.

Part 5

✥ Loving Unconditionally

Did you know that **if you love unconditionally you need nothing from anyone**? Unconditional love is so fulfilling that all we need is to love. It's amazing! Most of us don't understand love. We think of it as need and/or desire. But need is not love. Need is need. And desire is not love. It is a wanting for something that we think is missing. Nothing is missing. We believe that love is something we get from outside of ourselves, from someone else. Love is already within us. We are love. We have all the love we could want or need right inside of us. We just have to let it out.

We feel happiness when we stop looking for others to give us love and instead look inside of ourselves. To do this we have to give love unconditionally. That means <u>NO CONDITIONS</u>! We often think we are giving unconditionally, but then three weeks later, we're angry at the person we gave love to because they didn't thank us or respond the way we wanted them to. That is not unconditional love. Then we are in pain because our thoughts are not aligned with who we truly are.

Unconditional love has no expectations or obligations. It doesn't need to change or fix anyone. It allows the people in our lives to be exactly who they are. And it doesn't take the actions of others personally. Unconditional love focuses on "what can I give" rather than on "what am I not getting." It gives simply for the sake of giving. It doesn't evaluate whether or not the recipient "deserves" it. Besides, when we hold back our love from others, we are the ones who are missing out. We are missing out on an opportunity to feel incredible joy from within.

Don't hold back. Just love! See through the eyes of love and wisdom. When you look at others, see the beauty and perfection in them rather than the faults. Recognize that if they are behaving in unkind ways that one or more of *their* Five Underlying Causes are coming up to be healed. Love them for that. Tell someone that you love them and expect nothing in return. Just tell them because you want them to know how you feel. There's a difference between "I love you…???" and "I love you." One has a need and the other doesn't. When there is a need attached then there is always the possibility for disappointment and pain, and you will lose the feeling that comes with loving unconditionally.

<u>PAY ATTENTION</u> to how you feel when you love without conditions. You will feel fulfilled. Most of us forget to pay attention to how we feel when we are giving love. We only focus on how we feel when we're not getting it or when we're waiting in anticipation for the response that is going to make us feel good, the response that is only a temporary fix, the response that creates a need to constantly search for more.

Think about it. If you are walking around loving everybody and everything without any expectations, and you are noticing how terrific you feel when you do, then how could you possibly need anything from anybody? You are experiencing the love that you are. Try it! Feel it!

The funny thing is that when we're needy, we push people away, but when we love unconditionally and we no longer need attention from others, they want to be around us. Pretty ironic isn't it? When we love unconditionally, judgment drops away. We no longer feel competitive with others, nor do we feel cynical and untrusting. The world becomes a kinder gentler place and life is so much more peaceful and joyful. We feel inspired to serve others and give to our community and those in need.

So love unconditionally. It fills you up with so much happiness you can barely contain it; it energizes the happiness that is already inside of you. It is who you truly are. It is your natural state.

Part 6

✑ Using Relationships to Awaken Joy

We all dream of finding our true love, hoping that if we meet our perfect mate then we will be happy. So many of us look to relationship as the path to happiness; "If somebody loved me then I'd be happy." But another person cannot make us happy. Only we can make ourselves happy.

Looking to someone else to fill us with happiness is a tall order and a huge responsibility to place on another. Most importantly, it is an impossibility. Relationship can be a vehicle to awaken us to our happiness, but not by looking outside of ourselves and using the external temporary fixes we get from others as the path to our salvation and self-validation. It doesn't work that way.

Relationship is not a part of life for the purpose of gratification. It is in our lives for the purpose of revelation, to reveal us to ourselves. When we make a shift and begin to see relationship as an opportunity to learn about ourselves then relationship can bring us happiness. As we interact with the people in our lives, they are inadvertently giving us insight into ourselves. If we feel joyful around them, they are showing us our inherent joy. If they push our buttons, they are exposing our egoic patterns and pointing us toward our own healing. As the great teacher James Allen once said, "Circumstances do not define a man, they reveal him."

This is how it works. The people in our lives are just being the only them that they know how to be. We cannot change them, so it's futile to even try. Attempting to change or manipulate them will only serve to cause us pain. Nobody changes unless they feel the need. Those in our lives may be perfectly happy with how they are and have no desire to change. Or they may be miserable with how they are but unready to change. Bottom line is that we can't change them, only they can change themselves. Remember too that anything anybody says or does is about them, so anything our spouse or boss or family member does is about them doing what they believe will make *them* comfortable or fulfilled in the moment.

The key here is our reactions. What others say or do is not about us, but our reactions are. They reveal us. When it feels like somebody in our life has pushed our buttons, they are not the cause of our pain. It is our Five Underlying Causes and our Internal Teacher that bring up the pain. Claims such as "you hurt my feelings" or "you caused my pain" are false. Nobody else can cause us to feel anything. They can only bring out what is already inside of us. When we see this as an opportunity and begin to use it, then relationship becomes a marvelous catalyst for self awareness and spiritual growth.

Transforming Old Patterns

In order to bring out your happiness through relationship, you have to see the opportunity and act on it. Here's how:

1. Every time your buttons get pushed, remind yourself that the actions of others are not about you.

2. Remind yourself that they are doing the best they can with the tools and thought patterns they have. See through the eyes of love and wisdom.

3. Do not try to change their behaviors. You can't. Behaviors are the result of our thinking patterns, and only the people you are interacting with can change their own thinking patterns if they so desire.

4. Do not try to make them change their thinking patterns, as this will create resistance from them and pain for you.

5. Allow them to be who and where they are on their journey.

6. Take full responsibility for the way you reacted to them.

7. Acknowledge to yourself that the button that got pushed was your internal teacher giving you a message. Then explore the message by identifying your thoughts.

8. Recognize which of your Five Underlying Causes are coming up to be healed and then do the releasing and healing exercises (discussed in Part 2) to let those old patterns go.

If you go through these steps every time your buttons are pushed in relationship, you may even find yourself laughing at the pain, aware that your ego is really the cause of your discomfort and not the words and actions of another. This is very gratifying because you are allowing others to be who they are and because you are experiencing personal awakening. That is how relationship will bring out your happiness.

I was working with a woman who told me that her husband is very rude. Every night he takes off his socks and leaves them on the floor. When she asks him to pick them up, he does, but then the same thing happens the very next night. "He knows I don't like the socks on the floor," she told me. "Isn't that inconsiderate?"

When we awaken the happiness within us, words such as rude, inconsiderate, selfish and lazy fall away from our vocabularies. We discover that these are words that the ego uses to attempt to manipulate others. They are not the words of acceptance and unconditional love. What hadn't occurred to this woman is that maybe her husband doesn't have the same cleanliness needs that she does, and that taking off his socks feels so good that he doesn't even notice that they're on the floor. Having them picked up is *her* need. In going through the steps to finding happiness through relationship, she could identify that it was her attachment that caused her the pain and not her husband's behavior. He simply has different needs than she does.

Initially, her ego tried to convince her that if she accepted his behavior that she was allowing him to get away with something. But her husband is the man she fell in love with, and she knows the truth – that his actions never have an intention of malice. He is just being the best him that he knows how to be.

She can now make a choice: to accept him as he is, knowing that he will always leave socks on the floor, or to spend the rest of the marriage fighting with him about his socks and trying to change him. She can choose to take care of her own need and just pick up the socks herself, knowing that his habits are not about her. Or she can ask him every time he drops his socks if he will pick them up. If she sees through the eyes of love and wisdom, she will recognize where his behaviors come from. The one thing she can't do is force him to have the same needs that she has. So, she can accept him and stay with him, or accept him and leave him, but only through acceptance will she find happiness through relationship.

Authenticity in relationships will also bring out happiness. Don't say yes if you mean no, and speak your truth by honestly expressing your feelings. If you are always authentic, you will attract honest and trustworthy people into your life and you will have a greater level of intimacy in your relationships. Lack of integrity will always lead to pain and resentment. Don't be afraid to speak your truth.

Relinquish judgment. Focus on what you love about the people in your life rather than what you see as flaws. What you focus on you get more of, and what you choose to see in another will create your perceptions and experiences of that person. Love those in your life unconditionally. Practice the art of allowing. Let go of your attachments and accept them as they are.

People often ask if this will make them a doormat. If being at peace and unconditionally loving someone makes us a doormat then that's the kind of doormat to be. Nobody gets away with anything. The Internal Teacher takes care of that. Those who try to intentionally harm or take advantage of others are in pain, and nobody can be taken advantage of unless they agree to it. As Eleanor Roosevelt once said, "No one can make you inferior without your consent."

As long as you are always in integrity with yourself, you can never be a doormat. Sometimes being in integrity may mean that you have to leave a situation, but more often you will find that by looking at and healing yourself, what you thought was a problem no longer exists.

107

Being in relationship can give us two of the greatest gifts: the mirror into our own egoic patterns and the opportunity to love unconditionally. Sure we have to receive those gifts with grace and then act on them, but by taking action, yes, relationship brings out our happiness. It isn't always easy, because the old patterns and beliefs often creep in, but it is so worth it to do the work and to change the way we see and do relationship.

Part 7

༄· Conclusion

So, what is happiness and where can I get some? Happiness is a feeling that is already inside of all of us. It is not something we have to seek out or get because it is right there within all of us all of the time. We've always had it. We never lost it.

We can't get happiness from external things, although we keep trying because the temporary gratification we get from the externals gives us the illusion that they are making us happy.

Happiness is what we feel when we move away the cloud of thoughts that prevent the sun from shining through. We let it out by loving and accepting ourselves for whoever we are right now.

111

We are all on a journey, integrating our humanness with the Truth of who we are.

Love yourself for every step you take along the way of your journey. Appreciate the things you do innately that are aligned with Truth. Remember that beliefs create behaviors and that being hard on yourself will not make you better...and always be kind and gentle toward yourself.

See every situation as an opportunity. The painful moments in our lives can bring us joy if we see them for what they are – information. They are there to alert us to thinking that is not aligned with Truth. The painful moments are a gift. They help us to get back on track.

Acknowledge your Internal Teacher. It is giving you a message. Recognize the underlying thought processes that are causing the pain, and if you can, change how you are thinking. If you can't, then just embrace the pain as a message. Eventually, the observation alone will promote a release of old programs and patterns. When you see every moment as an opportunity and you act on the opportunity, you are constantly growing spiritually. This will bring out the happiness within you.

Say yes to "what is." One of the greatest causes of our pain is that we hate "what is." We think that we know better and that things should be the way we need them to be. But they aren't. Stop hating "what is." Accept the people and situations in your life. You can't change them anyway. You can only make choices about the way you react and respond to them.

Revel in the present moment. In Presence there are no problems. In the present, you are free of the pain that thoughts of the past and future create. You get all of the inspiration and direction you need in the moment you need it, and life becomes a miracle when you experience every moment fully.

Live in gratitude. Focusing on what you have will not only bring you joy, but it will bring you more of what you have. It will affect how you see the world and bring beauty into every day.

Love unconditionally. See through the eyes of love and wisdom. Focus on what is beautiful and perfect in everyone you meet. Give service to others without conditions or expectations and notice how spectacular you feel. Use your relationships as an opportunity to learn about yourself and to let go of the programs that have prevented you from enjoying life to its fullest. Practice the art of allowing.

Most people live from the outside in, always looking beyond themselves for happiness, past where the answer lies. Although the externals feel good for a while, the feelings always wane away. This is about living from the inside out, using what is already within us to experience our innate joy. This is something we can reach inside at any moment and pull out. No one can take it away.

This is where happiness comes from.

With Love –
Bonnie

Reference Guide

Practicing Self-Love and Acceptance

1. Make a commitment

2. Create a list of at least five things you love about yourself and review them everyday several times a day (say them with **_feeling!_**)

3. Add to your list as often as possible

4. During your daily life, focus on the things you do innately that are aligned with the true essence of who you are – love (stop taking those everyday moments for granted)

5. Practice relinquishing judgment

6. See through the eyes of Love and Wisdom

The Five Underlying Causes for Pain

1. We believe we're not good enough

2. We have attachments we are unable to let go of

3. We regret the past

4. We fear the future

5. We are not in integrity with ourselves

Steps for Turning Emotional Pain into Opportunity

1. Let go of all blame (that means no blaming yourself either)

2. Take responsibility for your own reactions

3. Listen to and acknowledge your Internal Teacher

4. Identify your thoughts

5. Identify which of the Five Underlying Causes for Pain are coming up to be looked at

6. Ask yourself what the payoff is for holding onto the thoughts and reactions that cause the pain

121

7. Embrace your discomfort by fully describing and then feeling the physical feelings in your body

8. Change your thoughts and perceptions

The Value of Practicing Presence

1. Presence gives you the ability to say "yes" to "what is"

2. There are no problems in the present moment

3. In the present moment, life is filled with miracles

4. Presence gives you all of the answers and inspiration you need in the moment you need it

5. There is no judgment or fear in Presence

6. Presence is surrender

7. Presence removes pain

8. Presence is your connection to All That Is

Practicing Presence

1. Use all of your senses to feel, hear, smell touch, etc... (don't think about it, just experience it)

2. Embrace the feelings in your body and fully feel them

3. Observe, without judgment, your thoughts as they arise

4. Follow your breath, putting all of your attention on the air moving in and out of your airway

5. Meditate

Living with Gratitude

1. Every morning and evening, make time to focus on what you have

2. Keep a gratitude journal

3. Be grateful for the people and opportunities in your daily life

4. Appreciate nature

Loving Unconditionally

1. Love without expectations or obligations

2. Allow the people in your life to be who they are

3. Don't hold back (when you withhold love, you miss out)

4. Pay attention to how you feel when you give love without conditions

Using Relationships to Awaken Joy

1. Remember that the actions of others are not about you

2. See through the eyes of Love and Wisdom

3. Never attempt to change another

4. Allow others to be who they are

5. Take responsibility for your own reactions

6. Be in integrity with yourself

7. Acknowledge that when your buttons are being pushed by the words and actions of others, that the Internal Teacher is giving you a message

8. Identify which of the Five Underlying Causes for Pain are being reflected back to you through your interaction with another

9. Use the Steps for Turning Emotional Pain into Opportunity

10. See relationship as an opportunity to bring out your joy and love and as a vehicle to help you recognize and heal the painful places inside you (relationship is a catalyst toward personal and spiritual growth)

What is Happiness and Where Can I Get Some?

Happiness comes from:

1. Self-love and acceptance

2. Seeing every situation as an opportunity

3. Saying "yes" to "what is"

4. Living in the present moment

5. Being grateful for what you have

6. Loving unconditionally

7. Living from the inside out

*Happiness comes
from within.*

Biography

Bonnie Moehle is an inspirational speaker, teacher, and writer. She is a graduate from the University of Health Sciences/The Chicago Medical School and the Southwest Institute of Healing Arts. Bonnie applies her education and spiritual wisdom in a career as a Self Realization Coach and Certified Hypnotherapist.

For over 20 years, Bonnie has been actively studying and teaching spirituality and alternative types of healing. She writes a monthly column for a Phoenix newspaper, facilitates workshops in and around the Phoenix area, and has a private practice in Phoenix. Bonnie teaches people to "be at peace and let their light shine."

133

To order additional copies of this book:
www.lifebalancingcoach.com
To book Bonnie Moehle as the Keynote Speaker
at your next event:
lifebalancingcoach@cox.net

Also By Bonnie Moehle

Thoughts from Within
A Guide to Inner Peace in Crazy World